VOICES IN THE RAINBOW

(POEMS)

NDUKA OTIONO

MACE BOOKS
MACE ASSOCIATES LIMITED

First published by Oracle Books Limited
No. 9 lbikunle Street Yaba, Lagos, Nigeria

First Published in 1997 © Nduka Otiono, 1997

ISBN: 978-33905-6-2

© Second edition 2021
Published by Oracle Books Ltd. in conjunction with Mace Associates Ltd.
1, Sanyaolu Street, Oregun, Lagos, Nigeria

ISBN: 978-978-8033-60-8

Permissions: notiono@gmail.com

Textual illustrations by Adenle Adewale
Cover art by Chuks Onwudinjo; Cover concept by Ochi Ogbuaku Jr.
Cover finishing and text layout by Ayebabelaedaipre Sokari.
Author's photo by Leo Solano

FORELINE

This collection can be seen as an experiment in *heteroglossia*, to borrow from Mikhail Bakthin. While sources of most of the allusions are intertextually acknowledged in the poems, others could not, regrettably, be traced at once. In the league of poets whose works benefit this project are five younger Nigerian poets of great promise: Chiedu Ezeanah, soul brother of the Obida fame, Sola Osofisan, Afam Akeh, Ogaga Ifowodo and Onookome Okome. Others whose voices also echo in this collection include Christopher Okigbo, Pablo Neruda, Gabriel Okara, Femi Oyebode, Niyi Osundare, Fela Anikulapo- Kuti, Bob Marley, Dambudzo Marechera, Tchicaya U Tam'si, T.S. Eliot, Fredrick Holderlin, Nikolai Kluyev and Nina Torn-Gangen.

Some of the poems in this collection were first published in the University of Ibadan Poetry Club Chapbooks. For permission to reprint them, I am grateful to the U.I Poetry Club. I am indebted to Harry Garuba, Sanya Osha, Ike Okonta and Pius Adesanmi for providing moonlight when the night seemed so dark.

I also thank E. C. Osondu, Editor of *For Ken, for Nigeria, The Post Express Literary Supplement* (PELS), *ANA Review, Quality* magazine, *Daily Times* arts and reviews pages and *Classique* magazine for introducing some of these poems to the public.

For love and for offering various forms of support, I am grateful to Onyi, my darling wife, my family and friends; to Etussy Abdulsalam, Ahmed Shuaibu, Joy Medu, Anthonia Okolie, Mike Jimoh and Pita Okute for logistical assistance; to Stanley Macebuh and Vincent Otiono, for material support.

(1997)

For this second edition of the book, I am grateful to: John Otu, for the insightful Afterword added to this edition; Nengi Ilagha and Chris Dunton, for editorial assistance; Fifi Edem, my publishing consultant for guidance; Chuks Onwudinjo, for the original cover art; Ochi Ogbuaku, for the cover concept; Ayebabeledaipre Sokari, for the cover finishing and book design.

I have taken the liberty of this new edition to lightly edit a few lines in this collection.

(May 2021)

VOICES IN THE RAINBOW

"There is a sense in Otiono's *Voices* . . . of diverse influences, currents wide enough to hold Pablo Neruda and longer still to include Fela Anikulapo Kuti . . . There's more than a hint in this collection of an eclectic spirit drawing from so many sources to etch his own vision with determined power."
—*ThisDay*

"Through this artistic experimentation the poet proves again the point that it is through a common humanity that a poet speaks to readers and listeners even in places and times other than his own. He comes out as a repository of communal memory."
—*The Guardian*

"In knitting a thread of images from. . .English and African modern poets and imagists, a delicately woven experimental work is produced. . .The language darts outwards. . .It smashes and soothes like the cunningness of the mouse that bites. . .Otiono's global view in this work is unmistakable, as is his sense of humour and of love."
—*Sunday Monitor Review*

"Otiono reaches his greatest heights when employing alluring images to illustrate scenes of daily life which though are bizarre in themselves, have become too familiar and therefore shed the nature of their sordidness."
—*Dapo Adeniyi, writer, film director*
and publisher of Position magazine

Otiono's uniqueness lies in his incarnation of the lilting voice of a raconteur and folk singer through which he transmits his message, and more so, in the expansive eclecticism of his allusions.
—*John Otu, Lecturer, Department of English*
and Literary Arts, Alex Ekwueme Federal University,
Ndufu-Alike, Ebonyi State, Nigeria.

To Onyi,

who intervened
in my sole journey
one so-long-a-night

CONTENTS

The rainbow they say is full of harmonies
—Christopher Okigbo

The highest genius is he who stands most
deeply in debt to mankind, who achieves
individuality by means of eclecticism
—Henry Wells

Phase One

DESERT CROSSING

You were a wanderer in my name.
and wherever you went you brought the settled folk
a little homesickness for freedom

—Herman Hesse

I
THE IMAGES TAKE WING

Here, where his body knew the earth,
In the antechamber of birth
Wherefrom he came with red earth innocence,
He comes again, a wanderer in search of the Word

Desert Crossing...

On the roadsides the images take wing...
Deciduous trees with leaves
Like the teeth of an electric clipper
Beautiful rock formation on Gwari road,
Designed like a ve-i-pee fence.
And lo!
White specks on the bough of a dogonyaro tree
Soon become jubilant cattle egrets,
Introducing the hillocks with bushy brows, near Tsafe...

Desert Crossing...

In the horizon inselbergs kiss the sky
With the 'innocence' of Judas
From the earth dust rises like wisps of smoke
The relentless intensity of the sun
Provokes sweat from the sweltering coal tar -
How mirages hug Macadam
With the fury of deserted gods!

Desert Crossing...

On the far side
A lonely vulture devours the putrefying carcass of a sheep
A tired camel defies his master's command
The thirst for water in the desert is the beginning of unwisdom

Desert Crossing…

Here's an oasis
The egret must drink, must bathe
The egret must bid farewell to dogonyaros
Whose trunks dare the desert to encroach

Desert Crossing...

An isolated transmitter towers in the sky
Challenging God, challenging man...
And the gullies appear again at deviant angles
Plains of arid soil stretch out like a woman on heat
Arguing with eternity, begging for rainfall
And still the desert sun tortures the brows of dogonyaros

Desert Crossing...

From the far side the huts emerge again
Rising from stony ground like yellowing mounds of hay
An old bridge pleads a case of *desertion*
In this season of lent
Paschal lamb anticipates their slaughter
And still the wanderer wonders,
The pilgrim laments:
"How far is home from these stones?"

Desert Crossing...

His lips are baked with dust
Not even the evening sun shines with leniency
As the sky hugs the soil in the horizon,
And the *Ustaz* offer prayers to Allah at Koko:"
ALLAHU AKBAR..."
Whose head is that shinning beside the praying ground?

Desert Crossing...

Underneath the flaming knife
The scalp hates the consolation of the fingertips
The circumcision knife hates the bleeding foreflesh
Here, passion is a scorched deciduous tree.

See: a hillock! a hillock!!

And herds of cattle forever foraging
Forever interrogating the hostility of the earth

Look: the ashen soil gives birth to anthills.

Desert Crossing...

Here is the river Niger at Yelwa;
there is the brook at Libale
And the birds flirt and flutter
With fleeting intentions of Valentine lovers,
The rocks! the rocks!!
Which rocks are, fertile?
Seduction lies in the distant coolness of night
And the night encroaches

Spreading its net of secrets
Over this long journey

Desert Crossing...

And the pilgrim journeys, and the images grow wings...
Silhouettes of rising ghosts
Sew wool over the traveller's eyes
"How far is home, wanderer?" they ask,
"These lines you jot down do they waltz to the rhythm of night?"
"Here, in the desert," replies the pilgrim,
"The taste of dust testifies to the 'innocence' of Judas

Desert Crossing...

In the horizon inselbergs still kiss the sky
Reminding the wanderer of the beauty in nature
Reminding that *Beauty is truth, truth beauty*

And the moments present themselves...
To stop and think,
To plough another mindscape...

II
THROUGH SCORPION-STINGS OF SUFFERING

Through scorpion stings of suffering
He walks, a pilgrim with swelling visions
Learning the wisdom of the chameleon
In a world where Oyebode sights

> *Unfostered orphans run on god's face*
> *run to grief, and decompose, guiltless*
> *on god's face*

Through narrow paths of night, he walks,
As the sun goes on holiday
For the moon to sing with smiles,
He remembers the parable of the Sower
And the fateful seeds of life
That fell on earth where asphalt formed crossroads
For the living and the dead to crisscross.

"THESE ARE HOLY GROUNDS!"

A steely voice erupts from the spirit world
The pilgrim turns,
And in the heartstrings of his mind
A medley of moonsongs twang
to scorpion stings of his down-beat journey.

'THESE ARE HARD TIMES!" says the earth...

The desert dust powders the pilgrim's feet
And there is no oasis to drink from

No oasis to wash his feet
But from the austere branches of a *lone* tree
A white bird intones Eliot:

*"What are the roots that clutch, what branches
Grow out of this stony rubbish? Son of man
You cannot say, or guess, for you know only
A heap of broken images..."*

In the region of darkling memory
Through pounding nerves of blood
Thought-steps sound at the pilgrim's mental anvil
As if there is no escape from the whips of chance.

Still he journeys through the forked, viper tongue of night
He journeys with his back bent with the will to survive
But there are no signposts on the moon-lit sky
No map to guide the pilgrim...
But there are times to stop and stare
At Nature's map of destiny on his palms
These are times he remembers his life
Drunk away in bottles of *kai kai**....

"PUT EVERYTHING DOWN AND RUN!" advises a poet.
"And be a coward forever?
Learn the wisdom of the chameleon and live!" exclaims the pilgrim.
"COMRADE, YOU ARE MISTAKEN.
THERE ARE NO TWO WAYS TO HEAVEN
ONLY THROUGH THE ROUGH AND WINDING PATH
SHALL THE RIGHTEOUS ENTER HEAVEN," argues the poet.
"Learn the wisdom of the chameleon and live!" insists the pilgrim

---

*local-gin.

...and with scorpion stings of suffering,
He journeys
Through narrow paths of a benighted life,
He plods toward He who'd promised:
> *"Come to me all ye who are heavy laden*
> *and I will give you rest!"*

RHAPSODY OF A LUNATIC

(For Ken, for Nigeria)

Let the wind rush
Crowned with foam
Let it call to me and seek me
Galloping in the shadows
                    —Pablo Neruda

I
RISING SONG

Who can stop these bullets of decadence
Flying in my country?

Who can heal these wounds inflicted on my homeland?

I wake up every morning
Thinking of sorrows, tears and blood...

I wake up, sweeping my lens across this terrain
Chained by tin gods and mammon, bullets and ballots

I wake up each day
Crying until a scarlet sun sets in my eyes
Mocking this plague that rules the nation

Who can heal this bleeding ulcer
Inflicted on my country's resources?

Who can deconstruct this art of madness,
Sons of a soil sodden with oil
But queuing for fuel at dry filling stations?

I plod thru the epicentre of this disfigured landscape
Frightening children with my ragged clothes,
Snapping shots of the characters I meet:

I see pain photostated
On the faces of starving citizens

I smell grief wafting
Out of the sweat-soaked under arms of poor labourers

And who can perfume this suffocating air
That reeks of sorrow, tears, and blood?

Stand by my side and look in the mirror with me
What do you see, raisins in the sun?
Or a sombre procession of:

Mourning widows whose husbands were washed with acid

Ageing children with a skin-thin spread of flesh

Truculent Area Boys and unemployed youths

Aggressive beggars praying for traffic-jams
So they could hustle for alms

Opulent politicians, khaki boys and dupes
Swelling inside automobiles of stolen comfort and vulgar wealth

Harlots dressed and smiling like
Models in glamour magazines

Writers and musicians searching for patrons,
Weary with worry over their next act

Compatriot, look at the far corner of my mirror:
Do you see honest people tempted to
Join *them* because they cannot beat *them?*
Do you know,
This is the hallowed slogan in our dear homeland?

Can you hear the humdrum of confusion at the bus-stops?

This is Lagos, brotherman, my morose mosaic;

My splintered image of madness...
Can you see these mottled images in the mirror?

If I disobey this surging urge to sear our shame
Will the Muse forgive me?

If my pen drips with bleeding lines
Would you blame me, soul brother?

I've seen sick men wail in the streets of this city
For want of chicken-change to save their children

I've seen mothers lost in men's thighs
So their children would survive...

And this is Lagos, *"centre of excellence"*!
Wherein I've learnt the tricks of survival like guerilla fighters.

"In the abundance of water, the fool is thirsty,"
Sings Bob, the legend.

Who can deconstruct this art of madmen,
Sons of a soil surfeit with oil
But queueing for fuel at drought-ridden stations?

If I shun this shame, my country,
Wouldn't our ancestors, citizens of by-gone happier days,
Wouldn't they denounce this song of the season?
Wouldn't they call it a madman's tantrums?
And you say a country deserves the leaders she gets?
Do you feel this grief grilling in my heart?
Can you hear me, avatars of lore?

Today, I sing of betrayed dreams, of raped resources
I sing of the hell that's here, the sanctions
That encroach, the angst, the dying flesh...

I sing of life and its profane abuse of all that's sacred,
I smart from insults on God by hypocritical zealots
Who eye heaven and abandon the commonwealth to rogues

If I disobey this compelling command,
This huge passion surging in my veins,
Nudging my heart to act, will you forgive me,
Lord? If I kill the exploiters, Lord, will you mind?

Use this Transition, O Lord,
Send down a messiah, not false prophets,
Not greedy Baboons!
Remove the savage desires lodged in the heart of the Rock

Let us sing of change, of revolutions that feed on human flesh,

Let distribution undo excess...
And when the Passover is over...
Let me sing of ornaments
To heal the scars of our rape and
Redeem the vestiges of decadence

But before the Passover is over
Let me embalm this shame,
Exorcise this mad umbrage
Into which I have been driven

II
GALLOPING IN THE GALLOWS

You should sing with Pablo,
My country people,
He sees you
Fermenting
Under the skin
Of my love;
He sees you
Sulking
Like dust
Before the rain...

And you say
You don't love me
Galloping away in the gallows,
Cherishing my presences
Hugging me in your dreams
Like the ferns
Encircling
A palm tree in the botanical gardens.

Sing with Neruda, sane folks,
For every moment
You see me,
Every moment
You think of me,
Your heart sings,
Your mind fractures into
Tiny pearls of envy for my freedom,
I, madman, citizen of the rainbow.

Son of man, you lie
When you say you don't care, you lie…
Your wishes betray you, smelling
Like damp forests,
Your wishes fly in the wind
Like confetti over a reluctant groom
Your wishes crave fulfilment
Like a bride
Anticipating wedding gifts,
Your wishes gallop in the shadows…
Prostrating before my maddening beauty…
Son of man, you care like Adam in Eden.
"Surrender now," says I,
"Macho man, surrender not," argues your Ego,
"Don't let you heart rule your head:
I've seen Samsons, have seen Solomons
In a common error (ask the Bible)"

Sing now, macho man,
C'mon, sing "The Captain's Verses":

"Let the wind rush Crowned with foam
Let it call to me and seek me Galloping in the shadows"

Sing on, New man,
Your voice
Booms
Like the towncrier's gong
Your voice
Baritones my heart
Like Pablo's lovesongs
Diagnosing the disease called Love

And you sulk with lust
Like dust

Before the rain...
Like the beast in you!

III
AFTER THE NOOSE

You sit inside the Tower of Babel
Looking at wanton hang men
Lost in a feast of hangings
And all you do is think of fascist repression
And of dark clouds
Gathering in the low sky...
Then you sing with the radio:

"Me I love my country
I love the land and people
Everything e dry for Nigeria
Make we join hands to make Nigeria better..."

No, No, No... sane folks,
Sing with Neruda, sing with Ken
Sing of poverty and the rape of the earth:

"Ah you don't want to
you're scared
of poverty,
you don't want
to go to the market with worn-out shoes and
come back with the same old dress"

Earthmen, you fear too much
Even wind rushes
Through your windows' nettings frighten you!
And you say you're sane?
I've seen women riot in Aba,
Damn the devil in uniform

Crucify his serpentine desires;
I've seen Amazons
Rout imperial lackeys in Dahomey
But you sit, watching
This generation suffer death by hanging
And you say
You love your dear homeland!

Sane folks,
I see you
Fermenting under a forest of flowers
I see you
Sulking with pain,
With hatred
For the dictator
Roosting in the womb of the Rock...
Rise up
Fallen heroes,
Rise up
Fallen martyrs,
Rise and take up your arms again
You who love this country as I do,
I, Madman, citizen of the moon,
Sing with me, sing with vengeance,
Wage war against the Baboons
Who pillage our barns

ESTRANGED! ESTRANGED!!

Alienated, you seethe with lust
Like harmattan dust.
You watch yourselves like mirrors
Cracking up like parapets of arid soil

And all you think of is "settlement",
An opportunity to share in the *loot*
And keep silent in the face of exploitation.

Sane folks, listen to the whirlwinds
Blowing across the nation:
Do you see new nooses dangling at the gallows
Do you see children dying from hunger?
Do you see citizens fleeing their homeland?
Do you see swords in the streets
Do you see the eye of the earth going blind?
Do you see despoiled creeks crying in the delta?

Country people, you lie
When you say you care (you love your country),
Rise, take up your arms
Against the mad man on the Rock.
Rise and muse with the poet of pendants:

"When shall I witness the violence
Of the poetry of my generation: this gift
That the times place upon our brows?"

IV
SOUL OF MY MADNESS

Bum rubber, burn.
Flames, infernos, burn...
Gas flares, scorching earth, burn...
My heart bleeds
Like May flowers of Pride of Barbados;
My words tease our inertia
As you say
Apathy is your name,
No longer Nana the toxic man
You amuse me
Like beggars hollering
Across tinted glasses
Of limousines at crossroads,
You amuse me, saying
I speak in learned tongues,
Alluding to Pablo the poet,
Baring our tattered lives before the world
But your pockets smell
Like the local cops' pockets!
Your palms itch in
Anticipation of another bribe!
Grubber, your name now is *Egunje*,
Your face, like the dictator's face,
Is corrugated with rust,
And I, poet of a hanged generation
Now chant with U Tam'si, the Congo man:

"You must be from my country
I see it by the tick
Of your soul around the eye lashes

And besides, you dance when you're sad
You must be from my country"

Burn rubber, burn.
Flames, infernos, bonfires.
Gas flares, scorching earth, burn...
Bare, burn their shame
Shell-shocked my heart bleeds

Like May flowers of Pride of Barbados
I'm your fucking madman
Tucking sanity into your heads

I'm brave
I rave
I read
I search for bread

I'm ostensibly mad
Sorrow in my heart
Tears in my eyes
Blood on my lips
Nooses in my dreams

I drink
I think
I mock
I truck about (singing Fela):

hungry dry waka for 'im face
        yeye rolling yeye
kalakuku kalakuku
        yeye rolling yeye

kuu kuku kukuku
      yeye rolling yeye
Yeye rolling yeye
      yeye rolling yeye

When I remember
How Ken's life was abridged
When I remember him galloping in the gallows
When I remember fragments of all I've seen, heard and read

I rap
I tap
1 rave
I crave revenge

I'm your ostensibly mad rhapsodist...
You amuse me
Pondering my monologue, wondering...
What manner of madness this is
I'm your wandering mad raconteur

I drink, I read
I brood, I parody
I drift, I craft my lines...

When I remember
Fragments, of all I've seen, heard and read,
I wash our dirty linen in the streets...

I rap I tap
I dance
I prance about

I laugh
I cry
I write my street poems
(Soul of my madness, monologue of my insanity...)

And ask not
If this be poetry -
Sojaboys killed the poet in me
Now I burn illusions in rhapsodies

Burn rubber, burn
		yeye rolling yeye
Flames, flares, bonfires
		yeye rolling yeye
Bare, burn their shame
		yeye rolling yeye
Look the man e dry waka
		yeye rolling yeye
Chant with Abami Eda himself
		yeye rollingyrye Kalakuku kalakuku
		yeye rollingyrye
Kuu kuku kukuku
		yeye rolling yeye
Yeye rolling yeye
		yeye rolling yeye

I'm ostensibly mad-
Sorrow in my heart

Tears in my eyes
Blood on my lips

I stomp
I romp
I read
I knead my pains

I, rhapsodist of an endangered generation
Sing of mapless journeys
Sing of landmines planted by goggled generals
Sing of fresh nooses on our darkling plane

Let the tidal waves rise
Roaring with Ken's legendary laughter
Let them rise
Foaming with the General's acids

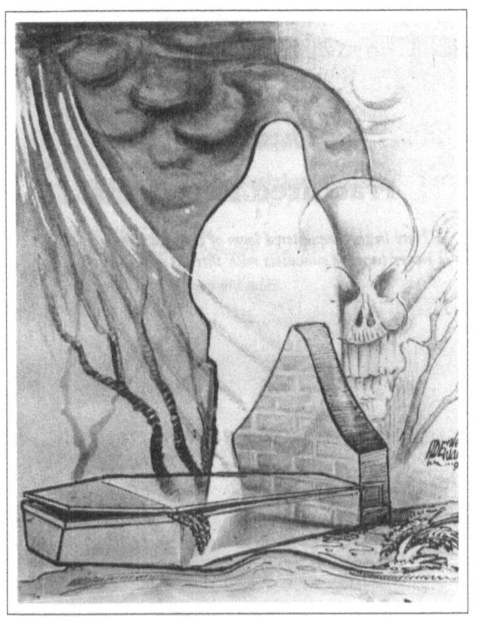

Phase Three

FRACTURED REQUIEMS

Here in this sequestered loom of textured shadows
I weave tangible silhouettes with threads of rainbows

DILEMMA

(To the rhythm of akele)*
Alternately—Crier, Chorus:

At the far side a funeral ceremony unfurls -
By the street corner a naming ceremony jostles

The smell of death rules the air -
The orphan-child marvels at the sight of the corpse

The coffin-maker pleads for more deaths
"The aroma of naira overpowers the smell of death," says he

The earth complains of skeletons
The morgue attendant celebrates another death

Our throats crack from singing dirges
Their necks bear synthetic garlands

We intoned: "Life's a terminal disease."
They retorted: "Life's a bag of fun!"

**Small drum, prominently used in funeral music.*

SYMMETRY OF A CEMETERY *

These columns of ageing clay white-washed
in sunny white renew the skeletons
of our deathly existence

As in this orchard of dusty humanity
spidery limbs roll symmetrical concrete
with immaculate coat of wastage

Leaving these white clouds on arid ground
to clothe the land with the cold logic of death
torturing our eyes with their symmetry...

But if the dead rebuke not this wild wastage
Dust shall reject this sepulchral painting

Upon witnessing the repainting of Ijebu Ode cemetery.

REQUIEM AT IBADAN*

(For Chiedu)

*To the rhythm of orimgba**

Now I hear the End Songs
My passion ruptures
In this chamber of creative chaos
Burning into pages of wisdom
Dumb as the tongue of an embryo
Savouring the kola-stained nights of lettered men
Heroes of a withering age...

Onwuka...

No sensations douse my instinctual desires
But plastic pains of battered sages,
Pastiches of half-suppressed songs
And the anguished memory of a 'rational' soul
Lost on a weekend in white cellophane bags of poison.

Onwuka...

Now I write this epilogue in our ancestral diary:
"The blighted weekend in Yuletide
Is for humankind to remember
To remember to mark the season
To mark the season with the
Unsung monotone of this Easter requiem
Sung to an insouciant soul

After a suicide report at the University of Ibadan.
Medium-sized drum used in funeral music.

Soul of a sanguinary suicide slide...
The blighted weekend in Yuletide
Marks the sententious trial of our fallen sons!"

Onwuka...

Did you say, "the lure of death is the juice of life
Confronting with the turgid passion
Of its hypnotizing child-like presence and
Ticktocking to the tune of shadows on our walls,
And fading with the fall of our magical future?"

Onwuka...

Here in this sequestered loom of textured shadows
I weave tangible silhouettes with threads of rainbows
Textiles of a brighter sun...

Here in this sprouting spot of careers
I struggle to master the logic in bald decisions and indecisions
I struggle to master the logic in bidding farewells to laughter

Onwuka...

"Here, we lounged lately
Romancing carcasses in this cemetery-cal earth
Listening to the tremulous threnody of sirens
Heralding vee-i-pees...

Here we rationalized lately.
Listening to the fractured requiem

Sung by busy bees working...
On days tolling the death of life-without-life
In this languorous season of End Songs
This torm season of Yuletides and Easters...

BEFORE THE BURIAL
(For John Okondu, R.I.P.)

Behind curtains of stains,
You wear shawls of death
Arguing the difference
Between the *tomb* and the *womb*

And you drove in evil hour, John,
And now we hum your requiem;
Remembering the fate of innocent men
Lynched at crossroads -

You wear shawls of death
Retreating with a bleeding scroll
Intoning an abandoned song:

My face is the buried horror
Of half-tamed human hyenas

Phase Four

LYNCHED ILLUSIONS

Now... illusions are lynched like hunger
And hope descends from the sky with anger
Like an old rag falling from a hanger

WHO CAN BLOW THE SMOKE AWAY?
(Okigbo Remembered)

Alternately—Crier, Chorus:

From faggots in the fireplace
The smoke uncoils...

No more sweetsongs no more lullabies
Only howls, only allusive elegies.

For the politicians are back:
The macabre dance unrolls like newsprint;

Who can blow the smoke away?
Who can prolong our laughter, prolong our lightening?

The eagles descend on us!
The horses neigh with anxiety!

To cast a vote or to cast a stone
"Already the future is mortgaged", cries the seer

And who can blow the smoke away?
Who can prolong our laughter, prolong our lightening?

As the smoke rises...
Who can lengthen our hopes, shorten our griefs?

Now the military maggots wriggle in *mago-mago** dance
The ill-bred politicians rehearse consensus dance steps

Ideophone connoting cheating, corruption.

Inside the foggy chambers of *wuru-wuru**
Power and wealth revolve like bolts.

No more lovesongs, no more lullabies
Only a rainbow of voices, rising from the tortured ribs of midnight

Sorrows metamorphose into tortured sensibilities
And Sola the poet explodes into darksongs:

> *"In my dear homeland*
> *If you're not a cobweb hugging*
> *A god's extended branch-work*
> *you belong in an unmarked grave."*

---

*Ideophone connoting cheating, corruption.

MONEY

(To the rhythm of cymbals)

Alternately—Crier, Chorus:

As dirt calls flies to parley -
So money calls men to corruption

As an equivocator that smiles and wails
So is money that which IS and IS *NOT.*

As a serpent beneath blooming grass...
And a wolf in golden vestments, is money

And as stale palmwine inebriates men
Men's eyes sparkle like mirror from money

As dust gluts the air like the sky's white clouds
So money gluts men's life like death

And as dirt calls flies to parley forever
So money calls men to parley with fever

LYNCHED ILLUSIONS

We journey through memories of forbidden coups.
The present conjures up images of the Medusa
Here the Ides of March...
No soothing inspirations
But the manic consciousness of prodigaled opportunities
And dreams fade into a series of errors of the paths not taken-
And the cruel realism of lost illusions imp-hinges imagination...

O ministrants, give us Freud and Jung
With all their wish-fulfilment theories
Here the collective unconscious is infected,
Every member of our membrane distends
From strains of living under siege!

Poet, did you say, *there're no people living here*
Only cannibals snarling over endangered species?

Did you say Niyi, where there is Hope there is Life
No longer where there's Life there's Hope?

O ministrants, O flute players!
Shall we make harmonies from hard times?
Shall we sing lovesongs with b-r-o-k-e-n voices?

Or, shall we write epitaphs for the giant in the cemetery...
Now that illusions are lynched like hunger
And *hope* descends from the sky with anger
Like an old rag falling from a hanger

"Tough times do not last,"
calms the optimist, "only tough people do."

But tomorrow another Andrew shall check out
Before the hike in airfares takes effect on April Fool's Day.

Here the Ides of March…
Though we may sing April Love next time,
Afam, life's no more the tutored tenderness of a lover

But the tortured sensibility
And the ping-pong smashes
Of lynched illusions and slow deaths!

MIDNIGHT VOICES

Hear the horn of the watchman by night
After midnight it is at the fifth hour
                                    —**Holderlin**

MIDNIGHT VOICES

(With flute accompaniment)

I

1st Voice (male):   let the choir sing in a babel
as this long column of the faithful reminds
me of the soul hunger
Dambudzo spoke of

2nd Voice (Female):   immaculate is the heart that thirsts for
the LORD
possessed the heart that yearns to kiss the
apparition,
her outline resting like a shadow on a
quiet mirror!

1st Voice: underneath the canopy of St Leo's Church
lo! long hands on the station of the cross—
white rectangle!
at her feet the faithful prostrate,

2nd Voice: touching her feet as if dipping
their hands in that wound on Christ's feet,
that wound drilled by irreverent nails of
crucifiers.

1st Voice: let the choir sing with a babel
life now is the rungs of a ladder,
for every step, a fall....

2nd Voice: and hour after hour after hour
there's no salvation from starvation,
no escape from wish fulfilment

1st Voice: and Lagos is swept by darkness,
and refugees prowl the refuse heaps
like cloudburst of darkness descending...

2nd Voice: as laughter is hidden in briefcases without briefs
and beads of tears torment the dilating iris
let the choir sing with a babel!

1st Voice: as the hours roll by, barefacedly
rolling with recollections of
Veronica's wisdom:
now, how many scarves will clean our tears?

2nd Voice: I can't see clearly now: those coming to worship,
how many are zealots, how many, harlots?
yet they insist: "No escape from the whips of faith"

1st Voice: "No escape from fears and tears of
Armageddon, and the choir must sing on
until the lights return ...

2nd Voice: and the red lamp shows the devil in red
                going.
                    going
                        down
                            Allen
                                Avenue...

II

3rd Voice (flute accompanist): Out of the crises our cry:

1st Voice: remove these temptations, O Lord!
let the steely will of *Job* prevail

for in this cesspit of temptations, evangelist
    Abodunrin*
assumes Jeremiah evangelist Abodunrin plays Daniel
evangelist Abodunrin assumes Thomas!

2nd Voice: shall we sing the Psalms, or shall we pray?
shall we ask Sammy* the boxer what happened?
within the lion's field faith and apostasy conjoin
"how will all this end?" asks the poet.

1st Voice: let the choir sing with a babel
questions of this sort need no answer,
at the opportune moment there's pleasure in anarchy
the new breed poli-trick-tian knows,
like Jesukayode*, the mystic

2nd Voice: between the indescribable violence of our time
between the rainbow of faith,
between this rainbow of voices,
dreams die, come through, die!

1st Voice: I'd rather leaf-through a forest of desires in the
sun than cast a vote for greedy misfits,
or count Africa's ribs with rays of hunger
    when the moon is out...

---

*Tried to tame the lion at the University of Ibadan zoo.
* Then a student of U.I.
* Jesukayode presided over a spiritual shop at Alausa, Ikeja, Nigeria, in the 1990s.

III

2nd Voice: let the choir sing with a babel
today the enumerators came,
counted Indians at the front flat and departed
forgetting me, holed up in the whiteness of my
        boys' quarters.

1st Voice: shouldn't I tell you, Ike, shouldn't I?
shouldn't they count our bones, count our throes?
should we sit through these lies the teevee tells?
shouldn't we ask the barracks dwellers:

3rd Voice: what do these voices portend?
do they really know there's great suffering in the land?
do they remember Christopher Okigbo & Nikolai
        Guyev at this crucial moment?
do they see the sky in rags, threatening with thunder?

1st Voice: shouldn't we ask, Akin" shouldn't we?
shouldn't we weep, shouldn't we bother?
whose blood is being donated, whose pain is
        harrowing?

3rd Voice: looking at the shadow, listening to the torrent
of questions:

2nd Voice: sing on choir, for salvation is afar
and the earth is aflame with false tongues
as they sing Hallelujah! Hallelujah! where's Handel?
where's the shepherd, where's the flock?

2nd Voice: sing on, sing on,
                with a babel, sing O choir:
                life is a rainbow of conflicts.
                before the shadow on the wall tell
                count O choir, O flute player count:

3rd Voice: how many beads are there on the rosary?
                how many beads of tears has hunger?

2nd voice: sing on choir, sing on
                for torn memoirs cannot hold the history of the
                children of Africa;
                recall the miracle of the fish and five loaves
                in this fateful cycle of destruction dance...

3rd Voice: now that faith is trapped in the desert wind, and life
                flutters like candle flames of Transmission,*
                who shall we complain to, Nina the poet?

1st voice: when Christmas comes and Koni, the lion, has
                sucked human blood, has drunk the evangelist's life
                        fluid,
                who shall we tell: "there is much suffering in life"?

2nd voice: sing on, charismatics, sing on:
                ring the bells with Nina, RING! RING!!
                offer her prayer for our lost souls:

---

*Controversial Celestial Church member, manufacturer of candles.
*Nina Torn-Gangen, late Russian poet.

"Blessed be the name of the universe!
Blessed be the call of life
Unchanging about us roll
The paths of unknown worlds,
But the heart - a red grain of sand
Is ringing out its reply
To dispassionate swarms of stars
And the tearful pleas of mankind."

TREASURED MEMORIES

in the depths of night
treasured memories brew and
are drunk in bottles...

of many nights of love
passed in bliss

of many nights of vigil
passed in the study

of many nights of anguish
 passed in unruly thoughts

of many nights of hope
wedged in the volutes of a hibiscus

but treasured memories
can not wrest

the bitter trespasses of
peregrinating dreams

along the lush veld of pleasurable sleep-
in the deep thighs of night.

NEW YEAR RAIN

through the torrential tears
of this New Year rain

      I glean...

in the sooty chambers of gritty earth
the amber colour of unspoken
litanies of love

      bordering...

the dying embers of fading memories

      whispering ...

"Love is a cloud of dust

      s-c-a - t - t -e- r - i - n-g

passion in the mystic loins of midnight."

"Oneness" by Salvator Onyeanu

Phase Six

SERENADES

And love is the pendulum in the clock of our lives

ASHES OF VALENTINE

Onyi,

this crucifix of ashes
branded on my forehead
this Ash Wednesday
rekindles my vows
in this season of *passion*
and bores through
like the crucifixion nails,
driven like the Love in the song:
so amazing and so divine,
it wants my soul, my life, my all

Onyi,

and the harmattan so dry...
the ashes and the dusts lash out
leaving the eyes red with tears,
the lips cracked and caked with thirst;
and I, griot of a threatened tradition
think of fireflies and unsung tales,
of starlit nights filled with heroic songs
far from the embers and ashes
of this age of decadence;
I, victim of an anxious generation,
think of Love and all that never fade.

CARIBBEAN QUEEN

(On the anniversary of her 21st Birthday)

(With guitar accompaniment)

Caller: Today...
I will kiss your lips that thrill with words
Hug your body that befriends my heart

Today...
In this pharmaceutical carnival of life
I will crave your company like solitude
Spell your name to the dulcitude of my new song

Anny...
In the thought-steps of this ode
Your name waltzes to the rhythm of my new song
Listen to the supplication of Our poet extraordinaire:

Chorus: *"O Anna at the knobs of the panel oblong,*
hear us at crossroads at the great hinges"

Caller: Hear, O hear queen of this Muse
Hear, O hear ageless mistress of the pool
Hear, O hear the minstrels' song
Hear, O hear the poets' gong
Hear, O hear the wisdom in Obida's observation:

Chorus: *"And already new tombs are being built*
Already new tombs are thirsty for children

Caller: Anny...
In this pastiche of meditation

I will caress your mind with words'
Share poetic thoughts in "Stolen Moments":

Chorus: *"Birthdays are hostile times to think about*
death- the fleeting life of honeyed moments,
death of dreams and all that flower"

Caller: Anny...
Twenty-one is a maiden's desire
When the shy giggles of puberty
Embrace the mature laughters of Motherline
When the innocuous babbles of adolescence
Metamorphose into the hard logic of experience

March on Anny, March on.
I will sing not "For she is a jolly good fellow"
I will sing not "Happy birthday to you"
But will sign your name on the vase of verse
Where the waves of fame shall wash it ashore
Where the agony of Time is the juice of poetry
And love is the pendulum in the clock of our lives.

O Anny of the brilliant blues...
Blessed are those who taste your delicious cookies
Chorus: *for theirs is the kingdom of constipation*
Caller: Blessed are those who taste the ore of pure love
Chorus: *for theirs is the kingdom of bliss*
Caller: Blessed are those who unburden their hearts
Chorus: *for theirs is the kingdom of peace*
Caller: Blessed is twenty-one, Anny, blessed be it
Chorus: *for it is the maiden's bank*
Where age like our signatures adorns the cheque of
adolescence!

Caller:
March on Anny, march on...
Today, I will emboss my love on your heart
Where Cleopatra shall not sail her vain barge
In the perdurable veld of this New Age
I will sign your melodious name on the blades
Of green leaves whispering poetry in the breeze:

Chorus:
Let wisdom be your burgeoning grass
chaperoned by these potent July rains
convulsing out of the ageless wools
above cooing out the blues of a God-sent dove.

Caller:
Anny...
Twenty-one is the crescent moon of life
Where ambition like Adam's Apple dangles
And maturity like libido tangoes

March on Anny, march on...
Let WISDOM disperse like splitting pods
And DREAMS thunder in the clouds
Where HOPE is the lightening that rends the night!

Anny...
Twenty-one radiates the colours of the rainbow
Caressing pregnant horizons
Mocking the sliding sands in the hourglass
Where Time is the lunatic watchman

March on Anny, march on...
In this season of rains
Let us shun cold like the bats daddy spoke of
And sit beside Time's tyrannical tree
Tracing our dreams in its roots.

Anny...
In this season of births and deaths
Let us cyst with love (hibernating)
Singing this birthday hymn
Let us remember Chidex (chanting)

Chorus: *"For, far away is the death that's near... "*

Caller: March on Anny, march on...
Listening to the *strained* melody of this song
    droning on and on
Let us dance with frayed nerves of joy
Zipping our hearts with true love
Let us mark with this soul - testament
The flaming 21st anniversary of your birth

And before the farewells, Anny...
Let us proclaim again with Obida,
Our *"seven-headed citizen of the rainbow:"*

Chorus: *"Do not abandon me, my song*
Like rain in pains
Erupt, utter the fates
And the tortures of my maimed graces"

PRIESTESS OF THE WHIRLPOOL
(For Yebo)

(With Marakas accompaniment)

rolling with boulders
through beds of running water
I come in search of you

priestess of the whirlpool
you shall swim with me
when the sea is safe

you shall swim with me
when the crocs and sharks have gone to sleep

you shall swim with me
when love is the wave that washes the sea

and you speak of worms
I know not how many earthworms
can feed a school of hungry fishes...
but I could pour libations
to appease neglected gods

I hear winds sing lovesongs
may whirlwinds be our music
may whirlwinds be our melody

come sing with me, windplayer,
in circles of the whirlpool
come dance with me, tender one
now the sun is a halo above my head
as waves break into lovesongs

WINDSONG
(Sonata for MEE)

(To the accompaniment of harmonica and tambourine)

I

Do you still hear the winds sing?
When you mock grief with your laughter
Ringing out of your heart of steel
Do you still hear the winds sing?
In the forlorn moments of crisis
When the world razors the soul with worries
Do you hear the winds sing?

MEE,

I've seen your eyes burnish like corals
Washed by the liquid flow of experience
I've seen your eyes burnish like brass
When all that's left is a challenge to shine...
Do you still hear the humanistic song of the winds
As you swim through life
Purveying tender tidings of a philanthropist
Do you hear the winds sing with wanton children?

II

MEE,

I've read your soul written into pages of light,
Written into luminous songs of innocent errors.
I've read new ideas arched on the bow of your lips
Each one an emblem of the struggle to triumph.

Do you still hear the song of the wind
When you speak of "Women Like Us"
And impearl my mind with feminine thoughts
Do you hear the winds sing?

MEE,

I too have walked thru broken images needling a terrain full of dust
Have smelt decadence in the fabric of our dear homeland
I too have heard the winds sing unbroken elegies
Have seen people lost in the circular dance of whirlwinds
Do you know,
When you play misty with your laughter
Ringing out of your soul wet with wits
I remember what the storm tells
I remember the lightening beyond the earth
I remember the challenges ahead...

III

MEE,

When the world razors the soul with worries
And you confront grief with your florid laughter
Do you hear the unbroken rhythms of Hope
Do you hear its whispering melody
Flowing with the winds like cumulus before rainfall?

MEE,

When the winds sing, resonating
With the swan song of existence
Do you sing with the wind in the forlorn moments of crisis

Do you sing: souls, blues and elegies
For this sonata is for you, is for us...
This
        Windsong
             is
                our
                   life!

LOVE SCANDAL

Like boils tormented by the hairy armpit
He ripened underneath the crimson sun of her love
Remembering the things they did on nights
When their ancestors' skulls exploded into orgasmic volcanos.

Within the ambit of fractured memory
Jenny's eyes constricted with hints of love
And her bangles jangled to the rhythm...
Of Boma Erokosima's* radio jingle,

There were times they sugared with infatuation
With vacuous emotions assuming the silvery colour
Of minted coins, assuming the powersaw edges
Of EI Anatsui's exhibits

But now the scorching heat of their love-scandal
Dissolves the sugary words banked in their hearts' vault
And her bangles jangle still...
But to the rhythm of their manacled - shame!

A popular broadcaster with Radio Rivers, Port Harcourt, also known as King of Talk.

APRIL LOVE
(With marakas accompaniment)

April comes, Gee,
and everywhere heartwinds
of nuptial knots threaten, birds
weep in porous nests for everywhere is
rain in tears,

here comes
the season of regeneration
of life and of love
here spreads out Easter wings
soaked in Ogaga's *Red Rain*
renewing our hearts
with the scarlet innocence of blood-knot

suck me in, ranting rain,
through the portals of the sky
suck me in,
for in the loving embrace
of your wetness
I breathe

my lungs on your fingers,
I inscribe
the crucifixion
of innocent souls on your falling arrows
shot from the heavens like Cupid's arrow!

April comes, Gee,
and everywhere

the heartwinds
proclaim April Love;
the heartwinds blow,
flying in my face

like the tendrils
of Palm Sunday;
the heartwinds whirl, Gee,
shredding my heart
like plantain leaves...

Gee, should I sing
with each rainfall
while you're out of sight?
Or should I trace
the graceful dimples on your cheeks
in this Easter poem
pondering
a marriage wish
curving down like the horizon
of my heart's walls
shouting
A-G-A-P-E!
this Good Friday morn.

Gee,
here comes
the season, of regeneration
of life and of love;
here weeps
the season of Christ's resurrection...
this is April, Gee,

a time to love, a time to live
a time to die with love emblazoned on our hearts
a time to ressurrect with joy...

Gee,
this is April, Eliot's "cruellest
month", this is April, a tribute to floral
beauty every where the earth. erupts
in new tongues
like a band of worshippers
drunk with expectations
of the coming Messiah.

Gee,
everywhere earthwinds
sing Hossana
in praise of Inspiration
which seizes the poets
but, Gee,
don't think poems come easy:
for every poem the poet dies,
he dies to endure like Easter passion

Gee, poetry is like
mating birds:
flapping and flirting wings,
sudden ejaculation,
and the seed
is sowed...

the clouds converse,
Gee, and every rain
the heartwinds of longing

caress the love lingering
in my heart,
the heartwinds of love
singing with whistling pines
like this rain in tears
tears my heart apart:
in search
of the promise
of Easter
I cry...

Gee,
here comes the season of rains
the season of regeneration -
of life and of love
of death and of revival;
here unfolds
the month of my birth,
and of Easter too!

Phase Seven

MOON DANCE.

in this corner of the earth, too,
life is a sad stammer
full of barbed-wire syllables difficult to pronounce

THIS EARTH IS OURS
(For Niyi Osundare)

(With drums accompaniment)

> *This earth is ours And the air*
> *And the sky*
> *We will defend them*
> —Fidel Castro

CALLER: Time shorn of wings totters through
              Crevices of rage and age, fame and name
              This earth is ours, son of Osun
              In the molten memory of poetry
              You mould songs that nourish the earth

CHORUS: *This earth is ours*
              And the air
              And the sky
              We will defend them

CALLER: Now laughters ring like forest echoes
              In your handshake with midlife, with fame
              This earth is ours, singer of tales
              You weave our toil and Our tears into
                      wreaths of laughter
              As imagination dances in mid-air like a moth

CHORUS: *This earth is ours*
              And the air
              And the sky
              We will defend them

CALLER: Laughter is a cruel exercise
           When the lung is bereft of air
           (This earth is ours, everyday bard)
           Laughter is a fragment of hypocrisy
           When the heart is laden with grief

CHORUS: *This earth is ours*
           And the air
           And the sky
           We will defend them

CALLER: Noma presents his bouquet of flowers
           At the crossroads of achievement
           This earth is ours, son of Osun
           When you crush experience into reels of laughter
           What do you tell the earth, songbird?

CHORUS: *"And the strength of our fear*
           Waiting, tail over head
           For the fear of our strength"

CALLER: We will defend the earth, defend our laughter
           Now that you name dances with toe wind
           Dances with the frozen letters of life.
           This earth is ours, weaver bird
           Now that your name is refrain in our song.
           Remember, O wordsmith, our bleeding scars

CHORUS: *"And the strength of our fear*
           Waiting, tail over head
           For the fear of our strength"

CALLER: Midlife is time to choose flowers
            From baskets full of thorns
            Still, this earth is ours, sunbird
            In the molten images of art
            We shall mould songs that nourish our earth

CHORUS: *"And the strength of our fear*
            Waiting, tail over head
            For the fear of our strength

MOON DANCE (LISTEN SYLVIA)*

they danced in the moon on nights
when the subtle shades of light in nite clubs
bewitched whores

and like crushed cocktail serviettes
they watched, consternation-struck, the poet
eat oil-bean salad with God's own fingers

they danced in the moon on nights
when the swivel chair hugged
the insanity of the poet lost in some frenzied creation

listening to what the typewriter said
with the bleeding vengeance of wounded words
on the tips of the poet's numb fingers

they danced in the moon
on nights when the Editor's
indecision intoned our friend's refrain:

*"Beauty is in the eyes of the editor.
The editor's indecision is final!"*

and they danced and danced and danced
shivering like high tension wires blown by a gale
until gales of laughter swept

---

*After Sylvia Plath's *The Bell Jar*.

the poet's lips trembling like their hips in orgasm,
trembling like the lips of a stammerer
before a difficult syllable...

O Sylvia, they still dance in the moon,
in this corner of the earth, too,
life is a sad stammer

full of barbed-wire syllables difficult to pronounce
life is a beautiful enigma
full of some lunatic's happiness in a lunar season

O Sylvia, they still dance in the moon,
in this corner of the earth, too, *the bell jar* rings
and life is a pus enjoyed by tin gods and mammon

WET DREAMS

Dreams come first

gentle like the nose
wet like the tongue
long like the oesophagus
pulsating like the heart promising like childhood

Dreams die last

dwarfed by realities
dried like a parched throat
illusory like a shadow resonating like breath
alive like death in ambush

LEVITATION
(For RMD, author of "I Know a Place")

hammering malleable problems
on the mental anvil of memory
orgetting the original act
nature ordered
at the toilet scene

    levitating...

SOOT' SAYER

this soot in the chimney
　　　of her lovely nose
sits like a soothsayer
　　　with harmattan's last
dust bidding my season of lust
　　　"goodbye!"

POSTCRIPT

June-storm exchange

First Voice: Like a leaf in the storm
I stumble through a forest
Littered with broken emotions
Bearing a covenant that binds the soul
And humming dirges to the whirlwind

Second Voice: Ah, this is a cross you must bear,
And you must totter
Through leaf storms of passions
Mixing memory and desire like Eliot,
Until the whirlwinds howl no more!

Lagos
June 1997

AFTERWORD

Euphonies Amidst a Medley of Voices[1]
By John Otu

My aversion to blanket globalization tempts me to begin this essay by interrogating the global context of Nduka Otiono's first collection of poems *Voices in the Rainbow* had the indigenous signifiers not been properly crafted. I could also have begun with the need to apprehend the traditional poetics of Otiono's collection but for the fact that I consider the book a practical performance of Mikhail Bakhtin's Carnival poetics[2] in particular, and a postmodernist sensibility in general. Paradoxically, *Voices in the Rainbow* is an inevitable arrival, a miracle born to consolidate the writer's immersion in the whirlpool of postmodernist discourse begun with his first book, *The Night Hides with a Knife*, without shutting out from its ambience the intractable lament about Nigeria's degeneracy.

A necessary analogy: on being published in the heat of WWI, T.S. Eliot's "The Love Song of J. Alfred Prufrock" was misconceived by some eminent literary figures like George Orwell as a necessary distraction, in fact, as a tract riddled with the aesthetics of levity at a time of momentous global crises. Of course, it is understandable that Eliot's contemporaries should apparently decry his thematic preoccupation and stylistic experimentation, what with the poet's seeming excessive concern with the bric-a-brac of daily living: "In the coffee room the women come and go / Talking of Michelangelo"; "I

---

1   This article was originally published in *The Post Express Literary Supplement* of November 22, 1997. p.9. The current version has been lightly edited with references added by the author. Dr. Otu is currently a lecturer in the Department of English and Literary Studies at Alex Ekwueme Federal University in Ndufu-Alike, Ebonyi State, Nigeria.

2   There is ample evidence in Otiono's poetics of considerable influence of Mikhail Bakhtin's discourses of polyphony, Carnivalesque, and heteroglossia in three of his seminal works: *Problems of Dostoevsky's Poetics, Rabelais and His World,* and *The Dialogic Imagination.*

grow old…I grow old…I shall wear the bottoms of my trousers rolled" (1973: 172), and so on. But unfortunately, Orwell was too concerned with the "serious" issues of life to behold the gem of bristling satire underlying that seeming vainglorious poetics. The inevitable question arises: could generation after generation have journeyed down the fountain of that poem to draw only on what Alexander Pope would call, "shallow draughts?" (55) Of course, not. In the modern era, poetry of eclecticism, allusiveness and intimations has been highly experimented upon by Ezra Pound in particular. Since then, the poet has broadened the canvas to encapsulate ramified cries and lilts of humanity to properly situate their angst.

From a superficial reading, some poems in *Voices in the Rainbow* (hereafter *Voices*) would strike the uninitiated reader as a work full of borrowings. Where is the author's voice, the reader may ask. Why the insufferable juggling of words and meanings? I hear the words and echoes of Tchicaya U Tam'si, T.S. Eliot, Langston Hughes, Pablo Neruda, John Keats, Afam Akeh, Fela Anikulapo Kuti, and a host of others, but why these intertextualities? The immediate answer to the above questions lies in the assertions of two great poets, Wole Soyinka and T.S. Eliot. In Soyinka's words, "A distinct universal quality in all great poets does … exercise ghostly influences on other writers—however different in background—at moments when a similarity of the particularized experience is shared. For the genuine creative mind, this need not be a cause for self-flagellation" (Quoted in Maduakor, 34). And in T.S. Eliot's (1951) words, "Immature poets imitate; mature poets steal" (206).

The strength of Otiono's collection then inheres in its dexterous execution of the carnival aesthetics, especially as posited by Bakhtin, a theory which intersects with post-structuralism and postmodernism. As one flips through the pages, one hears a medley which does not become raucous or strident, but jazzy; a complex note which nonetheless tapers off in an interesting euphony. It is necessary to note that Bakhtin apparently privileges heteroglossic or polyphonic image over the homoglossic or monologic. In doing this, he gives free rein to the myriad possibilities of a text. Hence, the emphasis on the dialogic or multi-accentuality of discourse, with no "appetency" repressed, to borrow from the famed poet and literary critic, I.A Richards. For this theory to work, the author's place in the text would be frozen to a barely perceptible signifier. Even this position is still susceptible to the buffetings of other characters' contrapuntal voices. Thus, as Bakhtin himself puts it, "the notion of individual identity is left problematic, 'character' is elusive, insubstantial and quirky" (Selden et al, 42).

But it is reassuring that even though Otiono works within the matrices of the carnival as well as the post-structuralist along with postmodernist schemes, the author's voice is not completely sublimated to the unstable trick of the text. It is significant that in spite of Bakhtin's exposition of the polyphonic accent of the text he still recognizes the controlling function of the artist in discourse. And, of course, this is unlike another important critic, Roland Barthes, who privileges the polyphonic text over the unaccented one. But like Barthes and Bakhtin, Otiono is enchanted by the libertarian language of the text rather than the monologic and, therefore, close-ended discourse. Hence the poet enthuses over what I consider to be the manifesto of his poetry.

> I drink, I read
> I brood, I parody
> I drift, I craft my lines… (p. 22)

Voices is replete with postmodernist intertextual devices: parody, puns, ellipses, humor and allusion. This makes the language largely conversational and the imagery local and familiar. The allusions to some aspects of the poems of U Tam'si, Sola Osofisan, Eliot, Okigbo, etcetera, are, in most cases, inspired and elegant. One finds the excerpts germane to the poet's themes. The two apparently distinct voices—those of the poets alluded to and our poet's—are blended in such a kaleidoscopic way that both interanimate each other. This is certainly a departure from Eliot's style especially in much of "The Waste Land" in which the reader can hardly find his way round the dense and far-fetched allusions and symbolism. In decrying the corruption that pervades Nigeria, Otiono aptly frames his lament in the poem "Who Can Blow The Smoke Away?" with the following lines from Sola Osofisan's *Darksongs*: "In my dear homeland/ if you're not a cobweb hugging/ A god's extended branch-work/ You belong in an unmarked grave" (*Voices* p.35). The poet becomes one with the reader, the native, given the speaking cadence of his voice, especially as he both playfully and seriously eviscerates the sorrows of the land. In charging the docile populace to forswear their enemies and pitch camp with the progressives, the poet's voice, laced with allusion to Saro-Wiwa's environmental rights activism and Neruda's social vision, regales us: "No, No, No…sane folks / sing with Neruda, sing with Ken / sing of poverty and the rape of the earth" (p.7).

Voices is an undulating terrain, a complex topography. Nothing is stable, everything is apparently in a state of flux. A reader is likely to be caught in a labyrinth: is the poet serious or is he trifling with his art? That is the object of a postmodernist text; to approach serious discourse through playfulness and humor. Thus, the collection is surfeit with counter logical images that capture not only the polyphonics of a Carnivalesque text, but also the poet's oral heritage and anguished soul. In "Caribbean Queen," for example, the subject Anny receives exceptional benediction from the poet: she is "Anny of the brilliant blues." But hardly had this praise epithet been given than it is cancelled out by a funny uncomplimentary addition: "Blessed are those who taste your delicious cookies/ for theirs is the kingdom of constipation" (p.53). Similarly, in "Through scorpion-stings of suffering" the pilgrim advises the poet to "learn the wisdom of a chameleon and live." But the poet counterpoints with "COMRADE, YOU ARE MISTAKEN, / THERE ARE NO TWO WAYS TO HEAVEN/. ONLY

THROUGH THE ROUGH AND WINDING PATH/ SHALL
THE RIGHTEOUS ENTER HEAVEN". (p.7)

The above stylistic strategy underscores the dialogic pivot
of *Voices*. No negative impulse or counter opinion is repressed;
everything is allowed to play out its extreme possibilities. That is why
in "April Love" the poet parallels the good with the bad: "this is April,
Eliot's "cruelest month"/ this is April, a tribute to floral beauty." (p.63).
In this light, it is clear that for Otiono, intertextuality does not just
approximate a corroboration of a precursor's contemporary idea or
style. It also implies a subversion and an interrogation. Hence, he goes
further to balance Afam Akeh's rose-bespectacled views about life in
"Lynched Illusions":

> Here the ides of March…
> Though we may sing April love next time
> Afam, life's no more the tutored tenderness of a lover (p.38)

It is remarkable that the poet resorts to Akeh's "poetics of tenderness"
in "Caribbean Queen" to celebrate Anny's 21st birthday. This, the poet
does because he seems intent on privileging a holistic view of life
over the fragmented, albeit through elliptical and multivalent voices.
Otiono would applaud Osundare for weaving "our toil and our tears
into / wreaths of laughter / As imagination dances in mid-air like a
moth," only to deconstruct him later:

> Laughter is a cruel exercise
> when the lung is reft of air
> (This earth is ours, literary bard)
> Laughter is a fragment of hypocrisy
> When the heart is laden with grief.
> ("This Earth Is Ours", p.67)

Otiono is deftly on a deconstructive mission; whatever is not whole (both in terms of health and completeness) is not worthy to be held up as a paradigm worth emulating. In doing this, the poet reminds us of William Blake, the iconoclastic Romantic poet, who postulates in his work *The Marriage of Heaven and Hell* that "opposition is true friendship" (xxv). Otiono also echoes William Yeats who insists in his radical poem "Crazy Jane Talks with the Bishop" that "Fair and foul are near of kin. / And fair needs foul" (n.p.).

Otiono's uniqueness lies in his incarnation of the lilting voice of a raconteur and folk singer through which he transmits his message, and more so, in the expansive eclecticism of his allusions. No reader should gloss over the poet's inexorable intent to strike a marriage between supposed opposites. In the repertoire of his poesy, every polarity between hill and hillock, whirlpool and melody, is bound to melt in the poet's alchemy and intriguing eccentricity. Hence, he further sings in "Priestess of the Whirlpool:" "may whirlwinds be our music/ may whirlwinds be our melody" (p.55). The question then arises: How can "Priestess of the whirlpool" swim with the poet "when the sea is safe" seeing that the calmness of the sea would rather attenuate her vibrancy? In yoking the two apparently disparate images together, the poet exposes the indeterminate and unstable perception of reality. Thus, in the poet's hands too, the sun loses its blazing tongue and becomes "a halo above my head/ as waves break into love songs" (p.55). Together, then, the most fervently resonating thesis in *Voices* is the uncanny welding of what hitherto were regarded as polarities. This is the poet's avowed job: to continue to bridge this lacuna until humanity learns to conceive of reality in wholeness rather than in fragments. His postscript captures this most aptly: "Ah, this is a cross you must bear, / And you must totter / Through leaf storms of passions / Mixing memory and desire like Elliot / Until the whirlwinds howl no more!" (p.75) But will the whirlwinds ever stop howling, seeing that even the core images of the collection are ambivalent? The rainbow is both a medley and a symphony. It is in the light of the ambivalent symbols and theme of *Voices* that one sees the collection as a scriptable or "writerly" text in keeping with Roland Barthes's theory in *S/Z: An Essay*. The reader can never be aloof to the jerky, rhapsodic terrain of the text. He has to intervene in order to appropriate some of the apparently flying signifiers that riddle the text.

The experiences concerning the brutal execution of the writer and minority rights activist, Ken Saro-Wiwa, and the decrepitude of the populace as imagistically depicted in the collection cannot be lost on a perceptive member of Nigerian interpretive community. But by a parodic and deconstructive twist in the poetry, which by every indication the poet is conscious of, there are no fixities in *Voices*. The symbol of rainbow is protean in the book: a rainbow of voices as well as a "rainbow of conflicts" which suggests that tenebrous unity is not achieved without anguish: "only a rainbow of voices, rising from the tortured ribs of midnight" (p.35). From the beginning of his exploration in the opening sequence "Desert Crossing," the impracticability of achieving a non-tremulous rainbow becomes clear to the poet. It dawns on him that the human mind is surfeit with "silhouettes or rising ghosts" which "sew wool over the traveller's [the poet] eyes" (p.5). It is in this light that the poet becomes wiser than when he first set out on his psychological peregrination. It is not in the inselbergs that kiss the sky with the 'innocence' of Judas, but rather, human beings and their fleeting existence symbolized by "the taste of dust" that "testifies to the innocence of Judas" (pp.5)—with innocence here used ironically to mean betrayal. The sum of the poet's discovery is that human beings are animals given to caprice and nothingness. But Nature is infallible as the poet invokes John Keats: "Beauty is truth, truth beauty" (Wolfson, 222) while seemingly concurring with Yeats' conception of reality as a "spume that plays / Upon a ghostly paradigm of things" (Ibid., 222).

A perceptive reader would reckon with the recurrence of the image of dust in many poems in this book. Notice should also be taken of the symbolic structure of the collection. The seven phases of the book correspond to the seven continents of the globe, thus giving bite to Otiono's global poetics. The poet, it appears, is not content to croon to an isolated clime, but to an all-encompassing performative resonance in which his country's woes are exceptionally highlighted. Consequently, the rainbow is both symbolic of musical harmony accentuated by the poet's use of accompaniments as well as the resources of songs and global harmony. As a pointer to this, the poet-persona describes himself as "madman, citizen of the rainbow" (p.14), and is also in turn described by the "Caller" as "Obida, our seven-headed citizen of the rainbow" (p.54). The seven-heads are mystically symbolic of the universe. And Obida, a revered stream in the poet's Ogwashi-Uku hometown in Delta State, represents its regenerative force.

Against this backdrop then, Otiono's poetics takes into cognizance the dissonance inherent in the clamour for globalization. Can all these disharmonies be woven into a stable symphony? the poet seems to ask. The poet further declaims: "O ministrants, O flute players! Shall we make harmonies from hard times? / shall we sing lovesongs with b-r-o-k-e-n voices?" (p.37) From the resonances of the poem, it is apparent that Otiono answers in the affirmative: There can be euphonies amidst a medley of voices; there can be melodies amidst poverty and dictatorship. From my reading, the poet seems to be of the view that in a global village, no clime, no epistemology should subjugate the other and that the uneven topography of the globe with the teeming discordant voices inhabiting it should be highlighted. Overall, therefore, *Voices in the Rainbow* strikes as a fine piece of work. It advances and consolidates the Carnivalesque and intertextual experimentation begun by the writer in *The Night Hides with A Knife*.

WORKS CITED

Bakhtin, M. Mikhail. *Problems of Dostoevsky's Poetics*, Ed. and trans. Caryl Emerson. Minneapolis: University of Minnesota Press, 1984.

———. *Rabelais and His World. Trans. Hélène Iswolsky. Cambridge, MA: MIT Press, 1968.*

———. *The Dialogic Imagination: Four Essay.* Ed. Michael Holquist. Trans. Caryl Emerson and Michael Holquist. Austin and London: University of Texas Press, 1981.

Barthes, Roland. *S/Z: An Essay.* Hill and Wang/Farrar, Straus & Giroux. 1974.

Blake, William. *The Marriage of Heaven and Hell.* Oxford: Oxford University Press, 1975.

Eliot, T.S. "Love Song of J. Alfred Prufrock." Kermode, Frank. et al (Eds) *The Oxford Anthology of English Literature* (vol 2.) London: Oxford University Press, 1973.

———. *Selected Essays.* Third Enlarged Edition. London: Faber & Faber, 1951.

Maduakor, Obiajuru. "Soyinka as a Literary Critic." *Research in African Literatures*, vol. 17, no. 1, 1986, pp. 1–38. *JSTOR*, www.jstor.org/stable/3819421. Accessed 19 May 2021.

Osofisan, Sola. "One Afternoon at a Roadblock." In *Darksongs: Poems.* Heinemann Educational Books Nigeria, 1991. 8.

Otiono, Nduka. *The Night Hides with a Knife.* Lagos: New Horn Press & Mace Associates Ltd., 2021.

Pope, Alexander. "Essay on Criticism." In *The Poetical Works of Alexander Pope Edited with Notes and Introductory Memoir by Adolphus William Ward.* Macmillan 2015.

Richards, I. A. *Principles of Literary Criticism.* London: Routledge & Kegan Paul Ltd, 1970.

Selden, Raman & Widdowson, Peter. (Eds) *A Reader's Guide to Contemporary Literary Theory* (5th Edition). Harlow: Pearson Education Ltd, 2005.

Wolfson, Susan J. *The Cambridge Companion to Keats*. Cambridge: Cambridge University Press, 2001.

Yeats, William Butler. "Crazy Jane Talks with the Bishop." Poetry Foundation. https://www.poetryfoundation.org/poems/43295/crazy-jane-talks-with-the-bishop Accessed 19 May 2021.

ABOUT THE AUTHOR

Nduka Otiono is an associate professor of African Studies and English, and Graduate Program Supervisor at Carleton University, Ottawa, Canada. Author and co-editor of several books of creative writing and scholarship, *Voices in the Rainbow* is his first collection of poems. The book won Honorable Mention for the ANA/Cadbury Prize for poetry.

www.ingramcontent.com/pod-product-compliance
Lightning Source LLC
Chambersburg PA
CBHW020132180726
47992CB00022B/2614